Yes We Can
But We Won't

Yes We Can
But We Won't

Lloyd D. King

To order additional copies of this book, contact:
Xlibris Corporation
1-888-795-4274
www.Xlibris.com
Orders@Xlibris.com
75089

CONTENTS

Dedication

*This book is dedicated to my parents and all of my other relatives
who are no longer amongst the living. They were my inspiration
and the very framework that molded me into what I've become today.*

*This book is also dedicated to my daughter and all the new graduates
who did their best and played by the rules only to find out
that the game has been changed.*

*I wish you all success and joy in your quest for independence,
and financial security.*

Personal Introduction

Hi, before getting to the topics I'm going to be discussing with you let me share some of my background information.

I was born in September of 59, the product of two loving parents. We started off at the poverty level, but my hard working parents worked us right up into the lower middle class (aka the working poor).

They were married for forty years, and then my moms got very ill and passed on. Five years later my dad joined her in glory. They both passed away relatively young. Neither of them saw sixty five.

As for me I'm 49. My occupation is an electrical construction worker. My life routine themes comes from a saying I heard long ago "Trust God, Clean house, Help others).

This book is being written because I'm mad as hell and I'm not going to take it anymore!

Chapter 1

Seizing Volcano

I've been laid off for to months, and there's no job prospect in sight. I live in Chicago it's August 2, 2009. Most of us tradesmen are hoping that we get awarded the 2016 Olympics bid. The Olympic bid has taken place and guess what Chicago was the first city voted of the process.

How did things get so bad? Ten years ago we were booming. Everybody was working. Hell I was picking and choosing my jobs. I was turning jobs down. Life was great not just for me, but for everyone else that I knew. We worked hard and we played even harder.

Shortly after the 90's we got a group of elected officials in power that changed the world as we knew it. One day there was a large surplus of money, the next day we were knee deep in debt.

The main person responsible for 9-11 hasn't been captured yet. We were told that the Iraq freedom venture wouldn't last long or cost too much money. We were even told that Iraq oil would pay for the war. Seven years later we are still there. It's going to be decades before we complete paying for the Blunder. That's if we ever get out of there. One week in spite of all the signs and warnings we were told things aren't that bad, our economy is in pretty decent shape. They said we are experiencing a few bumps in the road. We have a resilient economy. Don't get too worried about things.

Six months later out leading economic experts are reluctantly admitting that we are in a recession. Damn the word recession this feels like a depression. Lie after lie after lie.

Chapter 2

Education

The education system our youth are raised under
is another institution where untruths are practiced.

We tell our youth from day one go to school, do your best, study hard, and get a college degree. After that you'll start a good career, make lots of money and live happily ever after. I'm not saying that it can't happen, but let's teach that perfect ideal with a little more truth.

The school system should teach our youth that a lot of their good paying jobs have been shipped over seas. We should encourage our youth to develop their active imaginations. We need to teach them that they need to go to school for more than just an education. They should also be going to school to learn how to start and work there own businesses. We should teach our youth that formal education is only one part of becoming successful.

One needs to have that "I Can" competitive attitude. They also need to know the importance of good people skills, fair play, compassion and most of all honors in pursuing whatever there endeavors are. Then they'll be able to achieve success not only in the work force but also their piece of the world. They should be taught that the respect and admiration of fellow or business partners can carry them a long way also.

We should tell them how most businesses are relocating to countries where they don't have to pay a prevailing wage, or things like Medicare, unemployment, taxes, and other regulations that the U.S imposes on them to operate here.

The bottom line is that it is much cheaper for businesses to take their companies where they can pay someone two or three dollars an hour complaint free, rather than meet all the U.S impose regulations, pay taxes, and them hire someone that they must at least pay minimum wage salary requirements.

It's not like some people would say that our youth are falling behind and not smart enough to complete in the global work force. The cold hard fact is that these business people just don't want to pay our young working class college graduates the wages and benefits that they deserve.

Chapter 3

Crime Wave Increase

Being born and raised in Chicago, you kind of get use to people with a more standoffish aggressive nature. Most people stick to there own business, they live the old "I'm Cordial with everyone existence".

Lately there's been an increase in homicides amongst police related fatal shootings, as well as an increase in drive by related fatal shootings. I think we hold the record when it comes to school ages kids getting killed. Something's got to be done we need to stop this murder and killing nonsense right now. From both sides of the law.

Our society has become so desensitized to this violent lifestyle until it's becoming the norm to hear about teenagers killing teenagers. Innocent lives being taken by stray bullets, police involvement in excessive force cases, white collar thieves stealing millions and some cases billions from there share holders, politicians being caught accepting bribes, or people cheating on their spouses, church officials molesting the young boys in their congregation, teachers screwing students, the list can go on and on but for both of our sake I'll stop with that.

Back in the day when parents could discipline there offspring without being accused or called a child abuser we didn't have this many problems. Of course this rampant spread of drug abuse and alcoholism wasn't as prevalent either. I can remember doing something wrong at school and my teacher having no problem in disciplining me. Guess what, she told my parents exactly what she did too. I knew as soon as I got home that I would be getting another whooping for misbehaving from my parents as well. It wasn't just me that's how all of us were raised.

Even though we grew up under impoverished conditions there was a real sense of community shared in our neighborhoods. Teenagers played with teenagers, younger kids played with younger kids. If you were seen more than a couple of times hanging with those out of your age group, someone would confront you and ask what you were doing with them, and then tell you leave them alone! That was it everybody knew each other. Of course we had fights but that was as far as most of the incidents went. Two people slugging it out. No guns, no knives, just fist to fist. After the fight a couple of hours would pass and you would see the two fighters playing some ball together or walking down the street talking as if nothing had ever happened.

We were taught to respect every adult we came in contact with. None of that cursing and acting a damn fool because your folks weren't around. Someone always told when you did wrong and we always got punished for it. We would even get in trouble for disrespecting the block drunk, hell, he told on you too. What I'm saying is there was always somebody around that had the authority to correct us and then tell our parents what we did. The end results of living in a tattle tell society is less crime. It's better for us to disciple our children while there young, if we don't rest assured that the police or big Bubba in cell block C will when they get older.

Teachers could concentrate on teaching rather than living in fear about saying the wrong thing and getting there heads blown off. These new psychological techniques of child rearing just don't work for me. I realize that kids are people too. However, my main objective was not to become my child's best friend. My job is to raise my child to grow up and become a responsible productive member of society, whether they liked me or not.

Our children should be able to trust us and they should be able to respect us. My parents were very strict when I was coming up. I might not have always liked them but I always trusted and loved them. Now so more than ever.

As parents we should reward our children for there positive achievements. Give them a lot of opportunities to participate in different activities. Be active in there educational training, take a couple of hours a week for honest gripe sessions; teach them to respect themselves and others. Show them that it's okay to be an individual, and it's important to always do your best. Last but not least, if your child is hard headed and just plain defiant, the bible tells you that if you spare the rod you spoil the child (baring they don't have a medical problem).

We parent's need to take all the actions necessary to make sure that our children don't end up in jail or even worst dead. It's not easy raising kids these days, but remember they didn't ask to be here. So we have to roll up our sleeves and do the best we can with whatever we got. Our children will grow up, they will change. Sometimes the change is for the worst. If that happens we can have peace of mind just knowing that we have laid down a strong, solid moral foundation that they can always revert back to, if they want.

Chapter 4

Obesity Rear's its Ugly Head

Lately there has been a lot of talk about how American's are getting fat. Truer words have never been spoken. We hear about all of these low cal diets. We hear about different medications or pills that help people shred the pounds away. We hear about how important exercise is and needs to be done on a regular basis to slim down and stay in shape. All of those fact's along with countless unmentioned ways to lose weight and stay in shape will probably work. I don't condemn or endorse any of them.

What I will talk about is how our nation's food supply has been allowed to become so contaminated and toxic, till the end results of a normal person eating rationed portions might still end up with a weight problem. Most of our food supply is so full of steroids and different chemicals until you can't help but notice the changes in the physical appearances in let's say the youth of today in comparison to the youth of 40 years ago.

The kid's these days are bigger stronger and more developed by the time they reach 15 more than any other period in our history. Why? Because of the food!

Young girls are developing breast and beginning their cycles much earlier than before. The young boys are just getting bigger and taller, and noticeably more aggressive. Could it be that the same food that is changing the physical characteristic of our youth may also be responsible for the aggressive and fierce behavior that so many of them display sometimes?

Farmers are spraying the vegetables with insecticides, pesticides, and who knows what else to increase the size and quantity of crops that they harvest. I've seen seedless grapes, seedless watermelons, oranges the size of grapefruits, and grapefruits the size of small cantaloupe. I don't know about you, but something is definitely wrong with that picture.

I'm not saying that the food is harmful or dangerous. I'm just wondering if it's supposed to be that way. Crops are supposed to be rotated every so often. Purpose being is to keep the soil rich and full of various nutrients needed to produce healthy crops. I hear that in a lot of cases that might not be standard practice. Therefore a lot of veggies and fruits that we eat don't posses the nutritional value we think they do. Fruit or vegetables that don't contain nutritional value do not adequately supply our bodies with the vitamins and minerals we need in our system.

The farmers have guidelines tables limiting the amount of different chemicals they can use to feed their crop. I hope that those guidelines are being followed.

As far as livestock that we consume that's a whole different set of circumstances, filled with similar issues. Whose end results are similar to those mentioned in my talk on the fruit and vegetable dilemma.

Most of the livestock that are raised to be a supply of food source for the masses are being feed all kind of chemicals, unnatural food sources, steroids and so forth. Cows were meant to roam around freely. Grazing off of grass and other plant life that they like to consume. Instead of that there whole existence consists of them standing in one stall, where they are feed just about everything except what they were naturally intended to eat.

For the sake of keeping this book short and to the point, I will just tell you that poultry (chicken and other fowl) along with pork are raised under similar circumstances and share the same fate as that of the cow.

After they have grown up and are ready to be butchered, more preservatives and chemicals are added to the now dead meat to keep it fresh as long as possible. I've just given a generalization of the food sources process from beginning to end.

I'm not trying to discourage anyone from what they eat nor am I trying to give the ranchers and farmers a bad rap. The point that I want to make is: Americans are getting fat not only because of how they eat. We are getting fat because of what's in the food that we eat. The blame is not only in the hands of the consumer it's also in the hands of the farmers and food processors.

The best food source available these days is organic. Organic food however is very expensive in comparison to the counter part. That fact leaves me with a few unanswered questions. Why does it cost more to buy fruit and vegetables that supposedly is only watered, and grown with fertilizer when the none organic fruits and veggies preparation and growth process cost more.

The same principle applies to beef and other organically raised livestock (practically unheard of these days). But nevertheless when a supply of organic livestock is found the price is always astronomical and unaffordable by most of the population.

I'm aware that some preservatives are necessary to insure the seller that this product will be fresh when finally delivered for distribution. Beyond that, I don't know how much can grass and grain cost?

I went shopping one day and noticed that salami and bologna cold cut meats cost just as much as some cuts of beef and pork per pound. Cereal cost just as much as a package of sausage and bacon. From what I remember it didn't use to be that way. Our nation's food supply plays a big role in all of the sickness and disease we are getting ill with.

It's no wonder that here in the United States the healthiest people are the wealthiest people. That's not to say that if you aren't bleeding money you have to starve yourself to be healthy. But I am saying pay closer attention to what you buy, eat as much fruits and veggies that you can afford (preferably organic) and exercise. Don't go beating yourself up because you might be overweight, it's not all your fault but it is your responsibility.

Chapter 5

The Forgotten Ones

This topic covers a wide range of people, ideas, beliefs, and concepts. There are three groups of people that stick out to me as being forgotten.

Number one is our American Troops. These brave men and women risk their life and limbs to defend and reserve our constitution and way of life. Our armed services personal are unequaled with loyalty, braveness, and sacrifice for our nation. Our political leaders and lawmakers are quick to give praise and throw around a lot of rhetoric towards our troops. The only thing is that it's all talk. Our troops deserve more than that same old tired rhetoric of "I'm proud of you" or "We owe you a great deal of gratitude, thank you for your service to your country". Then after all of the B.S. they slap a piece of metal on their chest and give them a title. What a pathetic expression of gratitude. Instead of all that handshaking and rhetoric they should be given some real support.

Can you believe that they sent our heroes over there to fight a war without adequate safety gear and protection? The helmet and humvies needed to be altered and then to top it all I heard that some families and "real supporters of our troops" moneyed up and sent them (their family members) care packages which included better grades of safety equipment. It was even reported that the bullet proof vest weren't up to part. Where's the outrage, why weren't some heads rolling? Sending troops over there to fight without proper equipment and weapons seems pretty messed up if you ask me. How about you?

Our guys and gals are over there trying to protect other people's rights; they are helping to rebuild other nation's infrastructure, schools, responder buildings, and such the like. When right here at home our political leaders are limiting us the necessary capital to rebuild our own buildings and infrastructure. Our economy and infrastructure is in such shambles that we should be ashamed. The same fierceness and steadfastness that our troops display over seas should be displayed by the powers to be right here at home, to make sure that our troops have better to come back too.

There are no jobs, college tuition is off the hook, houses are being foreclosed on, crime is at an all time high and our Medicare system, well anyone that's alive knows the condition that it's in. Some of them are maimed, blind, shell shock, some are healthy and perfectly normal. Whatever the cost may be we owe out troops better.

They deserve more than the parade at the airport during their homecoming. They deserve more than the medals that's stuck on their chest. The VA administration and other armed forces programs should be funded and equipped with the best doctors. The most modern technology and helpful resources available. They should be given front line status on all jobs. They should be able to go to the closest medical facility near them and get the best care available on the governments dime. Modest housing for them and there family should be made available upon request. Also if chosen they should be able to attend any university that they qualify for on the governments dime also.

That's the way you say thanks to someone whose given there all in war and lived to tell about it. If professional sport people can make millions of dollars a year, if actors and actresses can make millions of dollars a year, if politicians can live like kings and queens, the least thing that the wealthiest greatest country in the world can do is fully support those who so bravely protect our way of life.

I'll bet you 10 to 1 if we paid our troops more and gave them a homecoming guarantee like I described, there will never be any need to even think about instituting a draft again.

2

Number two of the forgotten ones I want to discuss is our youth. Even as I'm writing we are leaving an unpayable bill left for our young ones to live up under. The power's to be have systematically set up all kinds of traps and plans to keep people in slave to debt.

Life is not only separated by race and ethnic background's it's also divided by economic conditions and circumstances. Those greedy big wig's are giving credit cards like a store gives out fliers telling about a 1cent sale. The college tuition level guarantees that most people graduating from a reputable institution are going to accumulate at least 50 to 60 thousands dollars worth of debt.

On top of that because of NAFTA and other under the table alliances, our children's education will become worthless (hello ain't no jobs.) A sizable amount of quality jobs have been shipped to countries that don't have out government regulatory safety codes, wage requirements, and tax structures to deal with. In other words "it's cheaper to run business in other countries where people work twice as hard for three times less".

The rhetoric about our kids not measuring up to world standards as far as education and work ethics are concerned is B.S. As far as I know people from all over the world still come here to get educated, and they still think this is the land of opportunity (this is where you can make big bucks).

So in essence we ought to make higher education more affordable. We ought to make it easier for entrepreneurs to start businesses. Tax breaks, various incentives, and loans given to foreigners should be given to American born citizens first. The interest rates on student's loans should be lowered. Special taxes should be added to American companies that choose to move over seas and get there products manufactured at considerable lower rates than what they would pay here but continue to charge ridiculously high prices to us for the merchandise. These extra taxes would in turn be used as scholarship money for those who wouldn't be able to afford college otherwise.

Admittedly this is a very complex problem and it's not all that cut and dry, however, the journey of a thousand miles begins with a single step.

3

The third group of people that are forgotten about are the hard working Americans that played by the rules and near the end of the game some greedy people stole all of their money.

What a travesty these are the people that are right at the retirement age, have raised families, and are looking forward to sitting back and enjoying the spoils of their labor that they save up, all of a sudden scandal after scandal and you know who gets stuck holding the short end of the stick they do.

Somebody has got to be getting paid off in the investment world. It's no way in hell that those schemes can get so big and go so long without someone in authority noticing. Locking the perpetrators up and giving them a fine is not good enough.

All three groups of people that I've talked about have tremendous obstacles to overcome. They can't do it alone. We all have our own set of problems and don't have extra out of pocket money for anyone. We do however have some time to call our lawmakers and lobby for them to add some new laws as well as change old ones, and maybe just maybe we can affect change enough to assist those who need it the most.

Chapter 6

First Things First

We have such a complex tax system until I won't even pretend to understand it. I know that we are spending millions and billions of tax dollars all over the world. Most of our tax money is going to the different war's that we are engaged in. A lot of our money is also going to rebuild those war torn areas that we destroyed. First we spend a lot of money to destroy then we spend a lot of money to rebuild, pretty smart huh? Like I said I don't understand it "the tax system" so I can't correctly speak on it.

This is however a subject that I can speak on. Our economy is in shambles and all of us have to tighten up our belts. Not because some one has told us to. We are tightening up now because we have to. The survival rules that apply to us for self preservation are the same rules that "should" apply to our government for self preservation.

My friend and I sat down and talk about what we need along with what we don't need during these difficult times. Shelter, food, utilities, clothes, emergency money, and money for the different medications that we take daily. All of those items are necessary for our survival. We can share a meal and maybe let someone sleep on the couch in an emergency situation, but beyond that the only things extra that we have to give is a listening ear and if asked some advice. Most of my advice is to tell someone to pray about it and let God direct them.

Back to our government. We spend billions of dollars all over the world, and during this crisis. its time for our government to cut back. We always here about how we have to cut back on what the politicians call entitlement and pork spending. I have never heard mention about cutting back on projects going on over seas. We don't hear them voting on cutting back funds to developing other countries. Our tax money is used to build new schools, fire and police departments, office buildings, infrastructure, also public and private housing. We give away hundreds of thousands of pounds of food, we build hospitals, and there are organized groups that supply volunteer services for teaching and health issues. They show people how to organize businesses. We even pay for private army services. All of the items listed above along with hundreds of others that aren't mentioned are paid for with tax dollars. The only thing to remember is that I'm talking about what tax payer dollars go to and supply overseas. Granted we so need to think global and help whenever we can. Key word is whenever.

When its time to talk about cutting back, I hope our politicians don't start right here at home. Let's lobby them to think outside of the box and first cut back on all that extra stuff earmarked to go out of this country. Let's keep our American family sheltered, let's keep us clothed and send our kids to new schools. Let's build new fire and police stations right here. Build new hospitals and let's invest in our infrastructure right here at home.

If our lawmakers would stop manipulating and trying to control foreign governments with taxpayers money, I'm sure that there would be more than enough to fund all of the programs we have in place here to help our under privileged citizens. Don't get me wrong I'm all for providing financial assistance or any other kind of service that might be asked of us during emergency situation in foreign countries. However, I am not in favor of giving any country a continuous supply of assistance especially when it short changes us right here at home.

Chapter 7

Somebody's Watching You

This part of the book will probably be the shortest. Our intelligence agencies are so damn intelligent until we don't know who or what is out there. I do know that our land and cell phone lines are easily taped into. I know that our computers and television monitors can be accessed and activated to watch you, without you even knowing it. I know that if they chose to target you, your every step can be watched both inside and outside of your home.

If you're an honest law abiding citizen our intelligence agencies are your greatest friends. However should you choose to live outside the law our intelligence agencies can be your worst enemy.

It's virtually impossible to gauge just how we are being monitored. Rest assured that it is happening. I am more for it than against it. When utilized in the right hands I know that it does more good than harm. That is why it is imperative for we the people to make sure that who ever is in charge, are the kind of people who are trustworthy with such powerful responsibilities.

People that have access to all of our most hidden skeletons have the ability to control. the intelligence agencies if put under the influence of the wrong people. They could be able to use leverage against politicians' which in turn opens the door for policy if not governmental control. Not only our government but other governments t as well.

Since we don't know to what extent our surveillance community reaches, lets make sure that the right people, who are for the people run the show. Even then it's a shot in the dark.

I say thank you and keep up the good work to our unsung heroes. Because of the nature of there job we will never know who they are. Hell they might work right besides you. Anyway, I salute our under cover agents and agencies for keeping me and our country safe. Without them and their sacrifices who knows where we would be.

Chapter 8

By Us For US

We are responsible for voting in judges, mayors, governors, congressmen, senators, aldermen, representatives, all on the local, state, and federal levels.

We listen to the prospective candidate's political rhetoric, campaign promises, we check out their personal and public background history, education, and family life. We should look everything over thoroughly before we vote for anyone. White, black, brown or yellow, it does not matter! If they abuse the law or our trust we should set them out of whatever office they hold.

Our elected politicians are not voted in office to represent big business lobbyist. For too long our views have been squashed because big money had a wider audience than we did and it should not have been so.

We the voters are the only ones who have the constitutional right to dictate and change policy. Not the President, Vice President, Governor, Supreme Court Judge, Congressman, or Senator. No one I mean absolutely not one of them has the right to decide anything regarding public policy making on there own.

They are to hold town hall meetings inform us of the topic on board, take a consensus on how we want them to vote and act accordingly. Granted everyone won't be satisfied, but as long as they vote according to the majority wishes they can't go wrong.

If the president makes a ruling that goes against the will of the majority of the American people, our elected senators and congress men are to vote against the presidents proposed action and shut them down. Especially when lives are at stake. They do have the power to do that and we have the power to make them do it.

There should be a limit as to how many times a senator or congressman can serve. Every one knows that power corrupts absolutely. Given enough time and enough leeway I bet you that all of those politicians in office would literally hang themselves. If left unchecked and unsupervised there's no telling how the big business, lobbyist would influence our elected officials. We need to help our elected officials by not giving them the opportunity to be tempted.

Limit there office terms just like the presidents two terms only then give someone else a try. Doing it that way would keep fresh people with new ideas representing the ever changing needs and views of our country. A lot of politicians that hold office for ages and for one reason or another get voted out. These are the same people that end up lobbying for big businesses. There ought to be a law against that open and obviously corrupt pattern. It's happens to often not to notice.

Remember everybody has skeletons and depending on how full your closet is as well as what's in that will determine how much another leverage another person has to use against you. They may even persuade you to vote their way!

I'm not saying that this kind behavior takes place in our nation's capitol. I'm saying that anything is possible.

Chapter 9

New Day

After all of the corruption, the lies, deceit, the total disregard for many of the American people wishes we got so fed up, that we voted Mr. Barak Obama to be our 44th president of the United States.

This guy came out of no where, one day he's a junior senator, the next day he is president. Let's look at the circumstances under which he was elected. After eight years of the G.W.B administration our nation's economy is in the worst state it's been in since the great depression. We spend billions of dollars monthly on war related responsibilities through out the world. The lies and deceit that got us in this mess is being swept up under the carpet. Our understanding of right and wrong moral behavior has been turned upside down. Even as I am writing our life's retirement saving and investments are being taken from the US. There is double standards one standard for your average citizen and another standard for your political leaders and the wealthy. The various groups for our elderly and underprivileged are being systematically if not totally eradicated, We are living in a world that says Americans are getting fat, yet funds are being pulled from our schools which forces them to cut exercise and fitness programs that battle obesity at the base level.

Because of the pathetic and unapologetic attitude help by the previous administration, other countries around the world despise us. We are looked upon as being hypocritical bullies who try to force there lifestyle on others and what's our solution. Elect Mr. Barak Obama to be our new president. Out of all the candidates that ran we felt that he could turn things around and get us back on track.

We were psychologically, spiritually, and physically beaten down so bad that we chose to think outside the norm. Then it happened, I never thought that I would live to see the day when the American people would actually vote a black man to be president.

All during his campaigning and even during his inauguration I was holding my breath, and watching T.V. with one hand over my eyes just in case something went wrong so I wouldn't see it.

Well it happened and he made it. There was new hope, a cool breeze or fresh air was circulating. We all took a few moments, sat back, and sighed with relief. For the first time in a long time we felt that in spite of the enormous almost impossible obstacles that needed to be overcome, somehow someway the Obama's administration would pull us through.

Some would say that Obama is the fall guy, meaning things are to far gone to be repaired and what's needed is someone crazy enough to put their face aboard this sinking ship then they can say "see there I told you those people can't do anything right!" "See how they messed up our country?".

There is a very narrow tightrope that President Obama is walking. I wish him success in all of his endeavors. If he is successful then we are ALL going to be better off. If he is unsuccessful then we ALL go down. I say to all of those who are unreasonably critical of this administration, be careful about what you ask for, you just might get it. Remember what happened the last time (G.W.B).

Chapter 10

Yes We Can

America with all of its different cultures was once considered to be the greatest nation in the world. Our reputation has been damaged, but it's not irreparable. We need to go back to the values that originally defined us. People used to make deals using only handshakes. Yes people were just that honest. At one time all they did was shake on it. Doctors use to genuinely care about their patients. It was not all about the money. Educators were in a class all by themselves. Highly esteemed and well compensated! Politicians well you know some thing's never change.

We were courageous, industrious, we manufactured our own goods, we farmed for our own country, and Americans supported America. We didn't start off relying on other countries to support us, why are we ending up that way? Greed, poor leaders and bad decision making is what got us in this mess. We have a new frontier with limitless possibilities it's called the green movement.

This is an opportunity for us to utilize new skills, search for better alternatives, form new companies, institute safer lifestyles. There is just no telling how far this new frontier can take us.

Let's change the way we go about doing business and try another route. We can be competitive and fair at the same time. We can work for a profit but do we have to make profit everything we work for?

The rich are getting richer and the poor are getting poorer. If we keep going under this same system we will all find ourselves going down the tubes.

History always repeats itself!

What goes up must come down!

The End